Fougeron Architecture

To Sophie, Jacqueline, and Pierre.

Foreword

Human beings have created various technologies that have extended the boundary of their own bodies toward the outside environment. Architecture, mediating between humans and their environment, belongs to this domain, but its relationship to technology seems uneasy. In various "tech styles," modern architects have represented technology within their designs to prove that architecture exists outside it. Interestingly, this process of representation tends to encourage the aesthetic of segmentation and articulation. The resulting designs make architecture unfriendly, using the nature of technology to separate human beings and their environment.

Unlike other technology-focused design, the architecture of Anne Fougeron explores the expression of technology without alienating the human body from the environment. Rather, it establishes an intimate relationship between the two.

Circulation and other functional spaces, such as the kitchen and bathroom, are arranged to form a building's spine, introducing a new order to the existing environment. Transparent materials or layers of glazed screens often envelope these spaces, creating continuity and fluidity while also serving as an interface that brings the changing phenomena of the exterior world into the interior. Temporal elements such as changing weather, seasons, and natural light are reflected on the surface of the screens, which are installed as tectonic elements with diverse textures and well-articulated details. Together, they create an animated materiality beyond the very material itself. As a result, the building's spine, surrounded by surfaces with various depths and reflecting ever-changing natural phenomena, enables various relationships between human bodies and the environment.

A similar attitude of integrating temporal elements as sensorial materials can be found in the firm's renovation projects, where aspects of existing buildings are incorporated as materials with temporal dimensions.

The architecture of Anne Fougeron explores the possibility of a new expression of technology while transforming it into a friendly mediator between human beings and the environment.

Hitoshi Abe

Preface

First, a confession: I'm obsessed with architecture. I can't imagine my life without buildings. And although this fixation can strain my health, finances, and stress level, I just can't give it up.

Like most obsessions, mine is driven by passion: the love and awe I've always felt for great buildings, old and new and anywhere in between. I'm also driven by the pleasure I have in designing them, in being immersed in the creative process and emerging in the end with a work that serves the greater good. As naive as it may sound, I do believe that architecture can change lives—both over time and in the moment. This is what fuels my passion. And at this point in my career, I increasingly appreciate all the architects, past and present, who have had the steely determination to express their own passions, who have taken the risk to confront society with their vision, challenging our ideas of what makes great architecture.

Le Corbusier, Chapelle Notre-Dame-du-Haut de Ronchamp, Ronchamp, France, 1954

Their buildings are never meek. Great architecture is provocative, demanding, intent on capturing our eye and informing our perception. For me, this emotive energy expresses the opposing forces that shape a composition: social and political, formal and structural, aesthetic and financial, material and natural. When an architect allows these forces to intersect with passion, to unapologetically break open a new design solution, the effect is vitality, not tranquility. It's pure power, realized through gravity and three-dimensional space—not just theory.

This is true whether the design in question is a small private home or a magnificent public building committed to a grand idea. The first time I entered the Hagia Sophia, for example, I was struck speechless. The passion of its creators, their vision, spoke with full force across time. And this power is also felt in emotional responses to modern architecture today: positive or negative, exhilarated or irritated.

Isidore and Anthemius, Hagia Sophia, Istanbul, Turkey, 537

Great architecture isn't about trying to please everyone. Sometimes it spurs heated debates among people who experience it differently. For example, my designs that bring traditional Victorian and bold modern elements into conversation with each other—forging a new creative vocabulary out of opposing historical styles—can seem like an argument to some or a satisfying dialogue to others. A composition that embraces and explores this complexity is the mark of the new modernist. What ultimately matters is the sincerity of critical inquiry and the level of craft behind the work.

My fascination with the interplay of opposites—with joining old and new, industrial and residential, rough and refined, urban and natural—began with my bicultural upbringing. Raised and educated in both France and the United States, I found a voice in more than one culture, more than one history, more than one set of opinions and aesthetics. My formal, visual, and social education was at the same time rigorous and liberating. I not only became familiar with and attracted to spaces with multiple readings, but I also became at ease working within different cultural norms, which has served me well as a feminist and non-conformist in my profession. As a woman architect, I continue to advance new solutions to design problems from a perspective that is, unfortunately, still very much a minority point of view.

My education also taught me to respect historic precedent, to develop an informed, critical awareness of art and architectural history, without excessive deference to it. In this respect, I align closely with art critic Rosalind Krauss, who argues that we are in the "post-medium" age. Now, the purity of art is what defines a work's "expressive power and historical contextualization," regardless of its particular medium.[1] It is imperative for great artists and designers to be knowledgeable and aware of the past and also willing to challenge its standards.

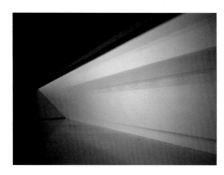

Robert Irwin, *untitled*, 1971

I believe this awareness of the past starts before any formal study of art or architectural history. It starts with the practice of seeing—cultivating different ways of seeing—and opening an investigative eye to the world. To be an architect you have to get out from behind your computer and look at real buildings, art, and natural sites. So much of modern life aggressively exposes itself to us, without a filter. The challenge is to critically observe this constant display with an interest that is both perceptive and demanding, selective and curious; to seek out the works of other artists and architects, from all eras, that intrigue and uplift us; to place ourselves in natural and built environments that move and inspire us; and to investigate our responses to them.

Dan Flavin, *untitled (Marfa Project)*, 1996

Through my travels and undergraduate study of art and architectural history at Wellesley College, I've come to admire a wide range of architectural masters—from Michelangelo and Borromini to Alvar Aalto, Le Corbusier, Kengo Kuma, and Hitoshi Abe. I've also found inspiration in the works of Mark Rothko, Dan Flavin, Robert Irwin, and Jim Campbell—artists who have shaped my way of seeing and thinking as profoundly as any architect. Irwin, especially, reinforces my perception of light as the most powerful definer of form and space. Along with Krauss, I see in Irwin's light-filled work a discovery of "the sublime, the absolutely great…what art opens onto when it opens up onto the world as perceived under certain optical conditions."[2]

Caravaggio (Michelangelo Merisi da), *The Cardsharps*, ca. 1594

Carl Nyren, Missionskyrka, Vallingby, Sweden, 1957

These conditions, as Krauss notes, are especially relevant in the vivid light of California, the location of much of my work. I'm always looking for opportunities to modulate the quality and character of natural light and to incorporate transparencies—both horizontal and vertical—by means of courtyards, skylights, glazing, or unusual types of glass, such as channel glass or dichroic glass. I interweave indoor and outdoor spaces with the interaction of light and dark, and like Rothko and Caravaggio, I'm fascinated with creating a sense of depth, even in flat surfaces.

In this ongoing experimentation, each project becomes its own investigation into how light metaphysically transforms a space—an investigation into light's ever-changing influence on our perception of space and well-being. I continue to explore transparency, both in the optical and the phenomenal/temporal/spatial sense. There's an exuberance in this manipulation of light and space that has universal appeal. The relationship between the optical and the phenomenal invites occupants to participate more fully with the environments I create, drawing them deeper into interaction with these spaces.

I enjoy provoking a strong response through a building's visual drama and multiple readings. Yet great architecture must also communicate humanity and balance. This balance rests on the material as well as the transcendental aspects of a building. All the details—materials, surfaces, and finishes—must exemplify the larger design idea. That's why I'm engaged not only in the theory of good design but also with its application: craftsmanship. Designing with glass and metal, wood and stone, and innovative high-tech and green materials, I've forged lasting collaborations with accomplished builders, craftsmen, and engineers. We brainstorm, we debate, and we solve problems in new ways. We each bring a different perspective to our public- and private-sector projects—but an equal passion.

Our creative experimentation for private clients has often become the laboratory for public-sector projects as well. Many times, my nonprofit clients with shoestring budgets initially aim for function and economy only. My job is to challenge those utilitarian notions by engaging nonprofits with the same high-level architectural ideas that animate projects for the wealthy. I strongly believe that the public sector deserves great architecture, that everyone of every income and walk of life deserves design excellence.

This is both a personal and political stand. In every project, the goal of Fougeron Architecture is humane modernism: creating environments that support the full range of their inhabitants' needs, their psychological and emotional responses to form and space, and their physical and social requirements.

Taking this design approach means crossing traditional boundaries and confronting old expectations within the field, pushing both our limits and the expectations and aesthetics of our nonprofit clients in stimulating, sometimes-uncomfortable-but-always-creative ways. I want the public environments we create to awaken all the senses and to uplift all the people who live, work, learn, and heal within them. Ultimately, I care most about how the inhabitants of a building will interact with each other and with the building itself for years to come.

Viewing architecture this way, with a social conscience and in the context of public policy, stimulates the most vital questions of design and democracy: How can we ensure that all citizens have access to the dignity and inspiration of great architecture? How can we purposefully broaden our profession so that breakthroughs come from designers of every gender, culture, and mix of aesthetic influences? And how will the buildings we create transform flawed environments for the common good and define twenty-first-century civitas? These are the questions that continue to fuel my passion for and obsession with great architecture.

Epigraph
Quoted in Friedrich Teja Bach, Margit Rowell, and Ann Temkin, *Constantin Brancusi* (Philadelphia: Philadelphia Museum of Art, 1995), 23.

1   Justin Wolf, "Rosalind Krauss," The Art Story Foundation, http://www.theartstory.org/critic-krauss-rosalind.htm.

2   Rosalind Krauss, "Overcoming the Limits of Matter: On Revising Minimalism," in *American Art of the 1960s*, Studies in Modern Art 1, ed. John Elderfield (New York: Museum of Modern Art, 1991), 133.

Acknowledgments

Above all, architecture is a collaborative endeavor. All of Fougeron Architecture's projects are made possible by the hard work of architects, designers, and consultants all striving to make better buildings. This book recognizes all the people who have worked in my office for the past two decades, particularly Todd Aranaz, who spent twelve years working on most of the projects in this book, and Ryan Jang, who is still here and diligently comes back to work every day.

Great collaborators and consultants include Dennis Luedeman, metal fabricator and much more; Paul Endres, a formidable structural engineer; and HTW, client and friend extraordinaire—you know who you are.

My special thanks to Princeton Architectural Press for their hard work and guidance in the production of this project.

Finally, this book would never have been possible without the exceptional talent, attention to detail, and intelligence of Ms. Bow—Clare Novak—who somehow manages to make sense and poetry out of my writing. I am forever in your debt.

Dr. Jekyll/Mr. Hyde: Modernism in the Traditional American City

A successful work of art is not one which resolves contradictions in a spurious harmony, but one which expresses the idea of harmony negatively by embodying the contradictions, pure and uncompromised, in its innermost structure.

—Theodor W. Adorno, *Prisms*

Theodor W. Adorno, *Prisms* (London: Neville Spearman), 32.

Pierre Chareau and Bernard Bijvoet, Maison de Verre, Paris, France, 1932

The new modernist interrogates the urban landscape with the critical eye of the Victorian flaneur, acting as both innovator and investigator of social forces. Yet this sharp inquiry never attempts to resolve the city's contradictions. The roughness of Mr. Hyde is now allowed to appear alongside the refinement of Dr. Jekyll.

In fact, the new modernist liberates all split personalities—old and new, public and private, interior and exterior—through rigorous yet idiosyncratic designs like the remodeled Maison de Verre. Embracing and heightening such visual tensions engages the city dweller's fascination with exposure. Acting as a form of the intriguing and incessant communication we crave, these designs allow us to see and be seen in multiple ways.

Thresholds change meaning in this world of ambiguous boundaries. Gone is the single entryway guarding a solid Victorian facade. The outer skin protecting our inner space now becomes translucent, admitting access to city and nature. Traditionally private rooms—where we undress, bathe, reveal—are now provocatively displayed. Even our horizons become playfully distorted by reimagined distinctions between ceiling and sky that challenge our perception of limits.

In each of Fougeron Architecture's designs, light acts as the transformational Jekyll/Hyde elixir, a form generator. It dissolves corners and walls, separates old and new, and revises notions of inside and outside. Entering not just through windows but from walls and surfaces above and below, light imbues space with multiple, changing identities, illuminating the complexity of modern life.

1532 House

San Francisco, California, 2006

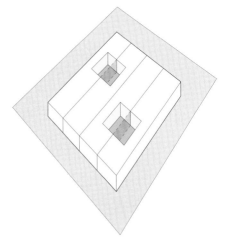

This new San Francisco residence and studio, infilled on a twenty-five-foot-wide lot, reverses the reading of the city's Victorian houses with a completely porous front facade. Its broad bay window intentionally invites passersby to look into the street-facing painter's studio and beyond—the sight line continuing through the studio and the three-story home in the rear to the backyard. Open slats replace siding, breaking the street wall while subtly echoing its rhythm.

The design incorporates two sectional moves. A horizontal one introduces a courtyard between the front and rear structures; a vertical one brings the ground floor, which includes the garage and bedrooms, down to street level. These two design elements create a powerful interplay between inside and out and between different levels of the house and studio. Light and transparency shape dramatic interior and exterior spaces.

This is a rare typology for San Francisco homes, whose lots are usually too shallow to accommodate an open courtyard. It promises a solution to a major problem in most city residences. Often deep and lit only from the front and back, they are invariably dark in the middle. On the contrary, the 1532 House has seven outdoor spaces, all with distinct qualities and views. Decks, walkways, and gardens unfurl around the living areas, heightening the visual complexity of the structure and its site.

The second floor of the house—an open floor plan with kitchen, dining, and living areas—is punctuated by a two-story staircase and is on grade with the backyard. The third-floor suite consists of a master bedroom, bath, and study. The bedroom's bay window opens up a spectacular view of the backyard and the city park beyond, repeating the form of the glass bay at the front of the studio, which captures a view of the Golden Gate Bridge.

The 1532 House is inseparable from its context. From every vantage point within, residents are visually connected to the incredibly varied urban landscape without.

opposite

Front facade

this page

top: Aerial view

bottom: Courtyard pattern

1 Deck
2 Living room
3 Master bedroom
4 Artist's studio
5 Garage
6 Street
7 Courtyard
8 Main house
9 Rear yard

Open ground
Open deck
Solar energy equipment

0   32'

opposite
Central courtyard

this page
Site, plan, and section

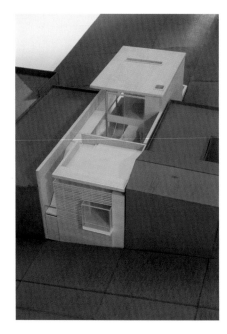
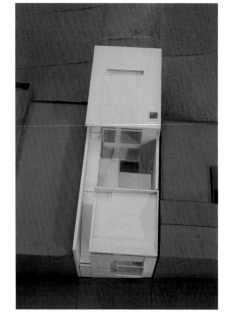
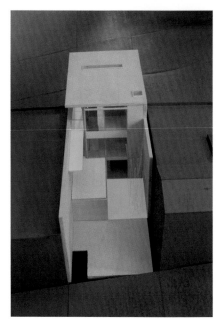

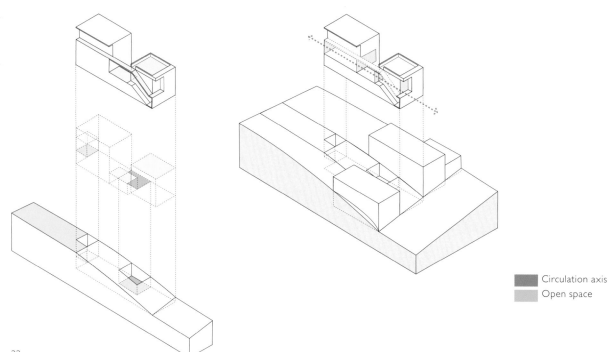

Circulation axis
Open space

opposite
top: Open-space studies
bottom: Conceptual diagram

this page
Master bedroom

overleaf
Living room

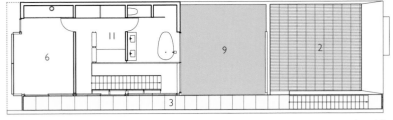

Level 3

Level 2

Level 1

1 Entry
2 Deck
3 Bridge
4 Living room
5 Bedroom
6 Master bedroom
7 Artist's studio
8 Garage
9 Courtyard
10 Kitchen
11 Study

0   16'

opposite
Bridge overlooking courtyard

this page
Floor plans

opposite
View along circulation spine

this page
top: Staircase detail
bottom: Weaving-rail inspiration: client paintings

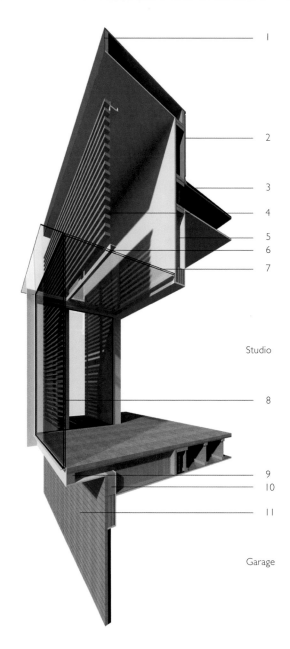

Studio

Garage

this page
left: Bay window and wood screen detail
right: 3-D rendering of bay window and
   wood screen detail

opposite
Front facade

1 Steel framed, built-up roof and metal fascia
2 Wood clad parapet wall
3 Roof deck
4 Wood screen assembly
5 Insulated wood framed wall
6 Metal L3 x 2 frame
7 Sloping glass roof and continuous stop
8 Insulated field glazing
9 Wood framed, cantilevered structure for bay window
10 Parallam at garage door head
11 Matching wood shiplap siding over facade and garage door

this page
Central courtyard

opposite
View from backyard

21 House

San Francisco, California, 2002

This remodel of a kitchen and bathroom in a San Francisco Victorian home explores the effects of transparency in both the optical and phenomenal sense. Exterior and interior glass walls allow light to create a continuously shifting reading of space that is dependent on the time of day. A glass box becomes the perfect layer of separation between the communal nature of the kitchen and the private nature of the bathroom. The translucent wall speaks of sensuality and voyeurism. During the day, light enters the bathroom from the south-facing kitchen, creating a bright, warm interior that accentuates the experience of bathing. In contrast, the translucent volume glows green at night through the use of jelled fluorescents, becoming a beacon for the gleaming kitchen.

Old and new are integrated without obvious historical or stylistic references. We reinterpreted the order of the Victorian house by aligning the front and back doors and creating distinct program volumes. Custom steel doors and sections for the exterior and interior glass walls convey the notion of craftsmanship and tectonics, linking old and new in a reciprocal dialogue.

opposite
Kitchen at night

this page
top: Street facade
bottom: Dining room

opposite
View along circulation axis

this page
New and old: bathroom stair detail

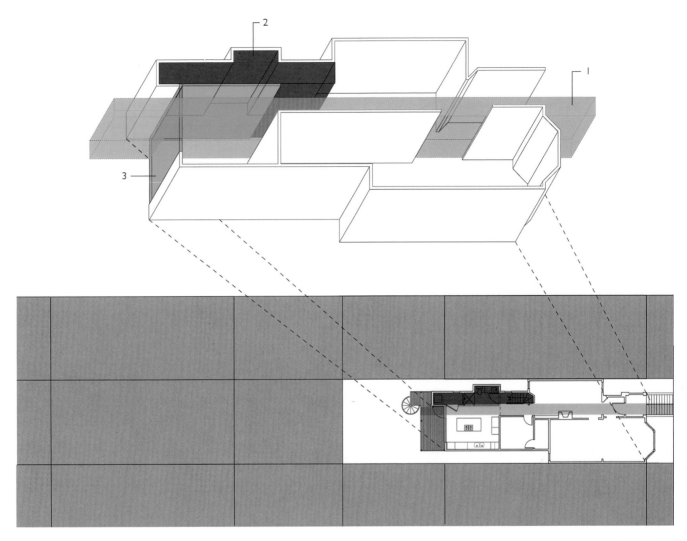

1 Circulation
2 Service
3 Transparency

opposite
First-floor bathroom

this page
Concept diagram

this page
Custom bathroom cabinets and vanity

opposite
Second-floor bathroom

View toward kitchen

440 House

Palo Alto, California, 1999

This new five-thousand-square-foot downtown Palo Alto home captures the opposing energies of Silicon Valley: the precision of technology and the exuberance of nature. Sited on the existing footprint of a 1950s ranch house, in order to preserve the site's spectacular live oaks, the two-story residence translates California's midcentury architectural vocabulary of indoor/outdoor living into a new modernist aesthetic.

The transparent living room volume exposes the front and back gardens to full view, both from the street and the interior. Open glass corners connect to the sky and the towering oaks. Private and public realms are thus dissolved to give primacy to nature, which defines the residents' fluid living space and invites the flaneur's eye.

The open-plan house incorporates the latest in building technologies, including innovative channel glass from England and avant-garde structural systems. In the circulation spine, the exposed steel moment frame, which provides lateral support during an earthquake and is made of thin columns and beams, expresses the home's construction system and its presence in an active seismic zone. Natural light from the floors, ceilings, and walls combines with translucent, transparent, and reflective materials—polished black granite, marble plaster, stainless steel, and silicon bronze—to create visually dynamic spaces.

Throughout, details and surfaces play with notions of formality and informality. The cool touch and reverberating sound of stone and glass in the high-ceilinged living room counter the warmth of wood and fabric in the cozy kitchen and den. All the senses are engaged in this modern dialogue of contrasts.

opposite
Central stair at night

this page
Brise soleil detail

overleaf
Rear facade

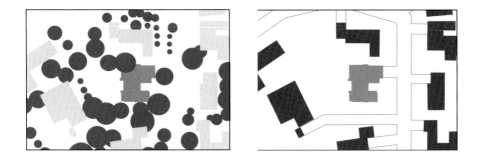

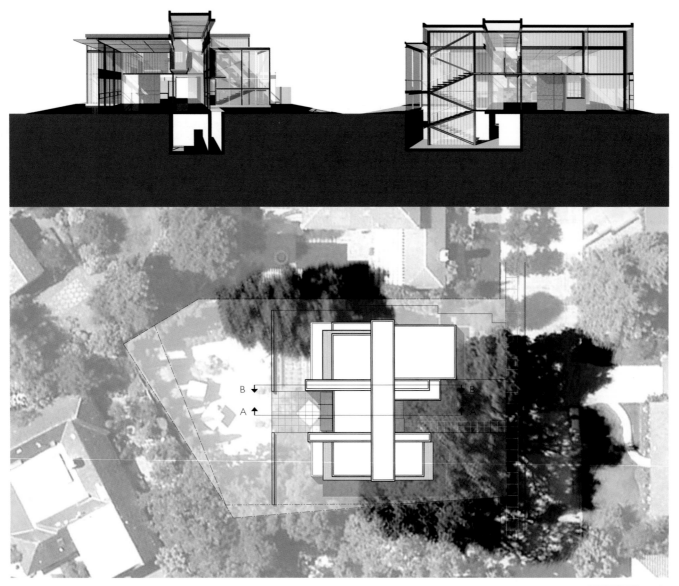

0   32'

opposite
top: Patterns of nature and street layout
middle: Sections
bottom: Site plan

this page
Main entry

opposite
Channel glass volume

this page
Central stair

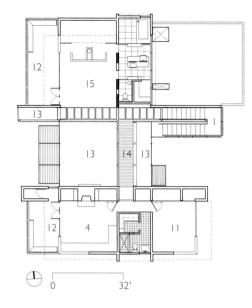

1 Circulation spine
4 Office
11 Exercise room
12 Deck
13 Open to below
14 Bridge
15 Master bedroom

0   32'

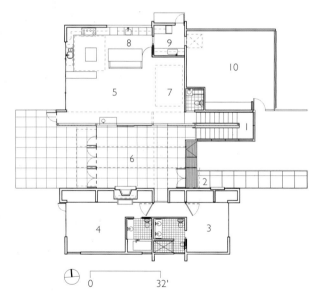

1 Circulation spine
2 Entry
3 Guest room
4 Office
5 Family room
6 Living room
7 Dining room
8 Kitchen
9 Mud room
10 Garage

0   32'

this page
top: Second-floor plan
bottom: First-floor plan

opposite
Living room

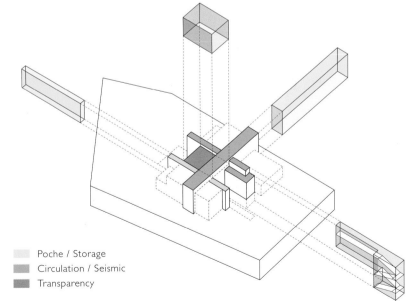

Poche / Storage
Circulation / Seismic
Transparency

this page
left: Second-floor bridge
right: Circulation spine and staircase
bottom: Conceptual diagram

opposite
Bridge overlooking living room

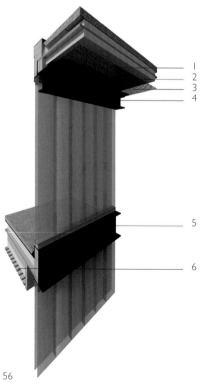

1 Metal plate
2 Exterior reglet head
3 Perforated metal ceiling conceals batt insulation
4 W5 × 16 beam
5 Web of W10 aligns with face of column flange
6 Wood slat ceiling

this page
top: Bridge overlooking living room (detail)
bottom: 3-D rendering of wall section detail

opposite
Living room

Fuel Lounge

Akron, Ohio, 2004

This sophisticated, modern wine and cocktail bar occupies a corner storefront on downtown Akron's Main Street, a conservative urban landscape undergoing slow and much-needed revitalization. The space was designed as a beacon, transparent to the street, attracting the attention of passersby and enticing them in.

The three-thousand-square-foot interior is divided into a set of spaces that flow into one another but have distinct, contrasting identities: a bar area over forty feet long, which is backlit with large etched glass and neon lighting; a room in front of the bar with couches and lounge seating; a small alcove behind the bar, forming a perfect place to see without being seen; two large turquoise seating pods with oversized wooden light fixtures; and VIP seating with padded fabric walls a few steps up in the back.

The sensuous palette of materials—a rich juxtaposition of woods, stone, glass, and colorful fabrics and furnishings—creates a space that is both edgy and sexy. The use of stainless steel in the tables, bar, and flooring reflects the client's other personality as the owner of a large steel fabrication shop. Even the industrial clips for the gleaming glass wall were manufactured there. The highly polished, stainless steel–clad columns also act as mirrors, giving patrons slightly distorted views of each other and themselves—a fitting play with point of view in this bar scene of altered self-consciousness. Projected on the glass wall above the bar are famous writers' memorable quotes about drinking—playful, ever-changing commentaries by literate voyeurs.

Main lounge space

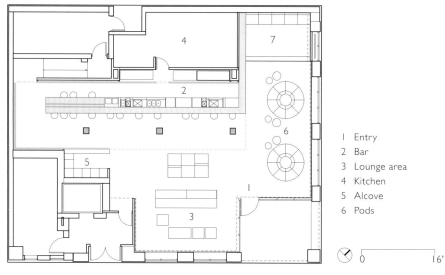

1   Entry
2   Bar
3   Lounge area
4   Kitchen
5   Alcove
6   Pods

0   16'

this page
top: Wall of dating: famous drinking quotes
bottom: Floor plan

opposite
Bar and wall of drinking quotes

opposite
View from bar toward main entry

this page
Bar from lounge space

Tehama Grasshopper

San Francisco, California, 2008

A surprising integration of old and new elements, of competing urban forces—industrial and residential, public and private, urban and natural beauty—brings this remodeled warehouse to life. The three stories of interlocked spaces have distinct personalities and functions: a ground-floor office, a second-level main living area, and a rooftop penthouse containing the master bedroom. The rigidity of the original concrete structure is broken down by a subtle interplay of light, surfaces, levels, and in- and outdoor spaces, making the urban living experience as richly textured as the city itself.

The new lobby of the ground-floor office space leads into a private residential entry with a custom steel staircase. This simple, unassuming entrance remains true to the industrial nature of the building and surrounding neighborhood.

The second floor is the main living space for the young owners and their child. A new open-air courtyard, cut out from the existing floor plate, connects the main living space to the new third-floor penthouse and the sky and is the focal point of their home. This vertical section translates loft into house, creating a hybrid of open-plan and conventional residential designs. Rooms are defined with translucent glass walls all around the open courtyard, bringing natural light and air into each, a feature more commonly found in house designs and not typical of lofts. This creates multiple layers of transparent views from one floor to the next, thus interweaving the in- and outdoor spaces with a play of light and dark.

The airy penthouse addition is the centerpiece of the design. The geometry of this sculptural object is a deliberate contrast to the orthogonal grid of the existing concrete structure. Suggestive of the rooftop staircase enclosures of old San Francisco warehouses, the penthouse adds natural form to the urban landscape—like a grasshopper settled lightly on the building surface. Its angular structural scheme, reminiscent of the opposing forces of the grasshopper's back legs and body, creates both a tension and a resolution of gravitational pull.

The penthouse living area includes the master bedroom and bathroom as one free-flowing space, which wraps around the courtyard, interweaving the upstairs and downstairs levels. Clear glass panes throughout—a requirement of the owners—offer no visual privacy, and the owners enjoy breathtaking views of the city skyline from any vantage point. Their connection to the outer world is a celebration of urban living.

opposite
Penthouse addition

this page
Grasshopper anatomy

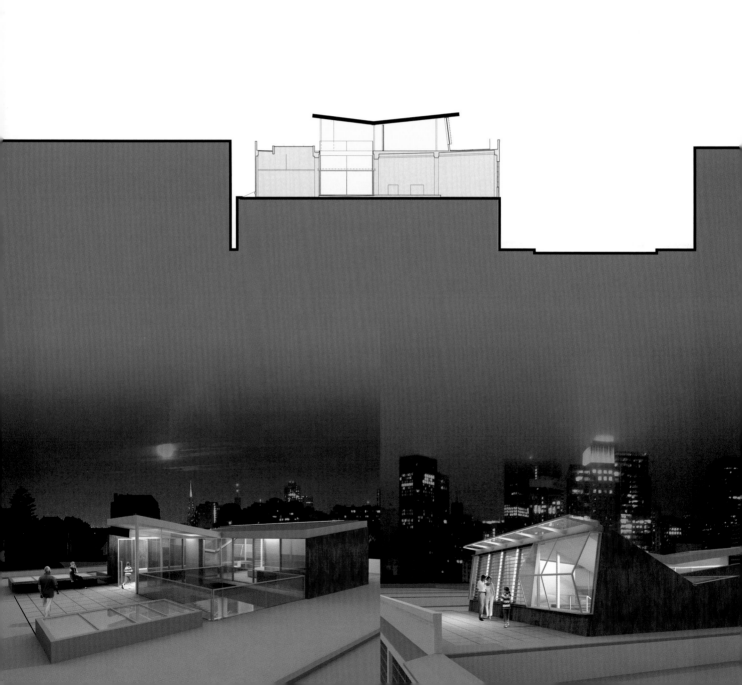

opposite

top: Transverse section

bottom: Night renderings

this page

View from across Tehama Street

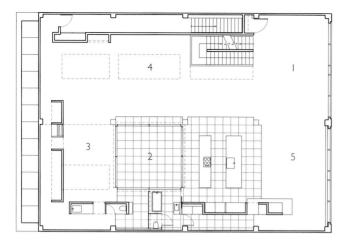

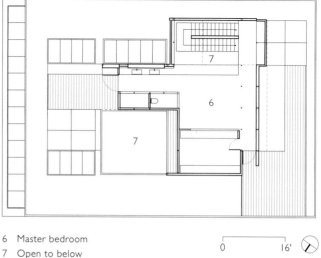

1 Entry from lobby below
2 Courtyard
3 Bedroom
4 Living room
5 Dining room

6 Master bedroom
7 Open to below

0   16'

0   16'

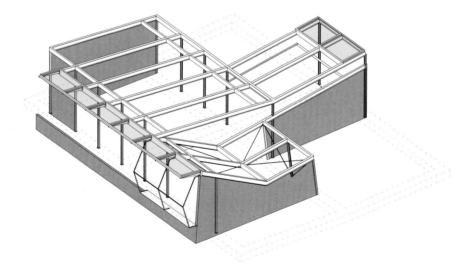

opposite
left: Second-floor plan
right: Third-floor plan
bottom: Axonometric structural diagram

this page
Master bedroom

top: Master bathroom looking north
right: Master bedroom looking south

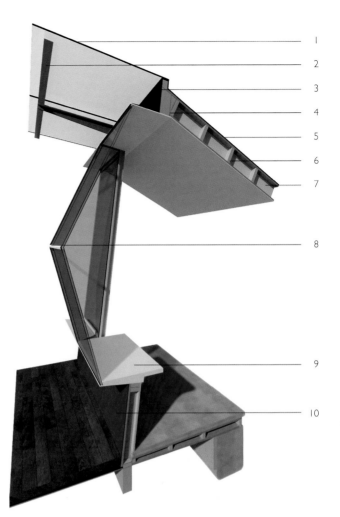

1. 3/8" safety glass
2. 3" × 3" steel angle
3. Sheet metal fascia
4. Header
5. Built-up roof
6. Wood ceiling joist
7. Rigid insulation
8. Continuous steel stop
9. Wood seat
10. Corten steel siding

top: 3-D rendering of wall section at
      penthouse stair
left: Bay window in master bedroom

opposite
Main stair to penthouse

this page
Courtyard and main living area

top: Dining room
left: Living room and penthouse stair

top: Central courtyard
right: Central courtyard from second-floor
    bathroom

this page
Kitchen from penthouse stair

opposite
Transparency: penthouse and main living area

Tension/Transformation: Forces of Nature

I placed a jar in Tennessee,
And round it was, upon a hill.
It made the slovenly wilderness
Surround that hill.

The wilderness rose up to it,
And sprawled around, no longer wild.
The jar was round upon the ground
And tall and of a port in air.

It took dominion every where.
The jar was gray and bare.
It did not give of bird or bush,
Like nothing else in Tennessee.

—Wallace Stevens, "Anecdote of the Jar"

Gunnar Asplund and Sigurd Lewerentz,
Skogskyrkogården Cemetery, Sweden, 1920

Placing form on wilderness is a radical act. It is not about creating harmony. Nature's tensions are too dynamic to be balanced and too sprawling to be tamed by human artifact. Instead, the dialogue between the jar and the ground beneath it, human artifact and nature, informs and transforms both, creating complex relationships between them.

Whether architecture treads lightly on or is embedded in the land, the new modernist first looks deeply into the forces that shape a site: climate, topography, geology, light, vegetation, and wildlife. This context is then reshaped by structure, which demands that nature surround it. Independent and yet interconnected, the form and its environment challenge and confuse each other: Which is greater? Which is more in control? Which will last longer?

The architect amplifies these questions without answering them, using the forces of nature to inspire the forces of design. Nature's efficiency, its evolution of form and function, its graceful geometry that gives living things poise and strength, are all conceptually applied, not copied, in the structure. The result integrates human presence into the wild in a way that invigorates both.

And in these structures, people come to the land in a new way. Protected and sheltered, yet exposed and engaged, they too are challenged by a new modern experience. They do not retreat to nature with an illusion of serenity or dominion. They enter nature with a clear view of its original power.

Jackson Family Retreat

Big Sur, California, 2005

Steep canyon walls dominate this wooded site next to a creek in California's Big Sur region. When the owners first commissioned us, local governing agencies were intent on leaving the land as it was—overgrown and uninhabited. However, working with ten consultants over three and a half years, we satisfied all the requirements necessary to build a modernist 2,500-square-foot two-bedroom family retreat here.

The structure sits lightly on the land, respecting the ecologically fragile nature of the site, and is precisely attuned to its forces. A formal object in a natural context—like Stevens's jar on a hill—the house holds its own in this tall, cavernous place, neither dominating it nor dwarfed by it.

The building is composed of four volumes made of different interwoven materials that create visually and spatially complex exterior and interior spaces. The main volume, clad in standing seam copper, runs parallel to the canyon. Its thin butterfly roof sits delicately above a band of extruded channel glass, connected to the roof structure by thin rods that are invisible from the exterior. These rodlike columns, which become wider as they go further down into the walls, are used to lift the entire structure two and a half feet off the ground, reducing its impact on the land. At both ends of the house, two-story clear windows frame views of the redwoods and the canyon ridge, bringing in vistas of the sky—sunny by day, starry by night.

A one-story volume in the front half of the house comprises all of the service functions—cooking, bathing, washing—while a custom steel-and-glass volume at the back opens to views of the creek. The fourth volume, the staircase, clad in stucco, acts as both the house's seismic structural brace and a visual foil to the shimmering, transparent volumes floating around it.

The plan explores the tensions inherent in family getaways: open areas for communal living; private spaces for solitary retreats; and outdoor expanses for relaxation. A combination of transparent glass and extruded channel glass reflects and dapples the light throughout, creating a dynamic play of brightness and shadow.

Living room at night

overleaf
top: Site plan
bottom: Site location within canyon

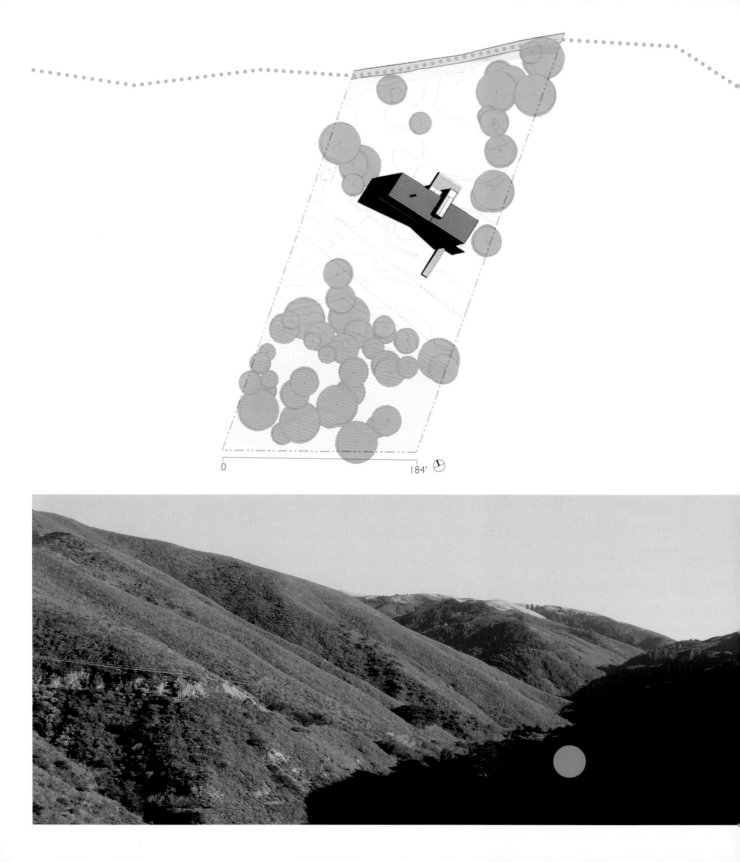

0   184'

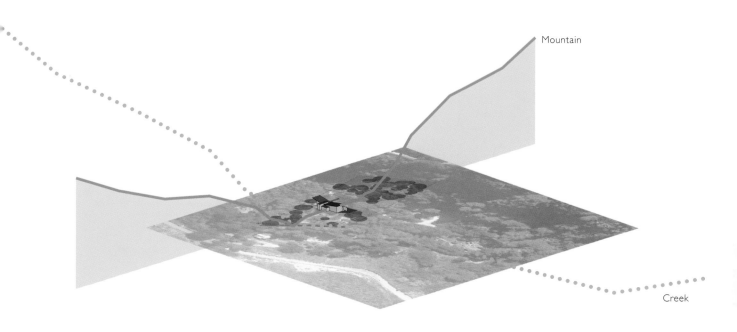

Mountain

Creek

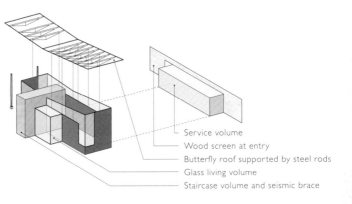

Service volume
Wood screen at entry
Butterfly roof supported by steel rods
Glass living volume
Staircase volume and seismic brace

top: Second-floor roof deck

previous spread   bottom: Structural and conceptual diagram

Front facade   left: Rear facade

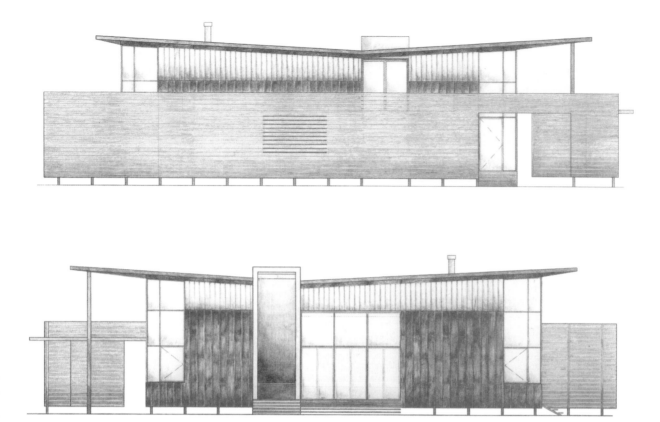

this page
Early hand-drawn renderings in colored pencil

opposite
Rear patio

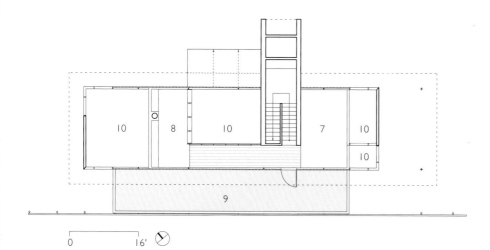

```
|———————————|    ◐
0          16'
```

7 Sleeping loft
8 Library
9 Deck
10 Open to below

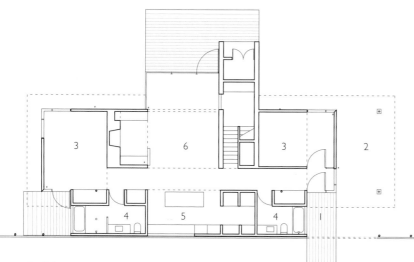

1 Entry
2 Carport
3 Bedroom
4 Bathroom
5 Kitchen
6 Dining room

this page
top: Second-floor plan
bottom: First-floor plan

opposite
Living room

top: View to master bedroom
right: Kitchen and bridge from living room

opposite
Library overlooking living room and inglenook

this page
Library and bridge

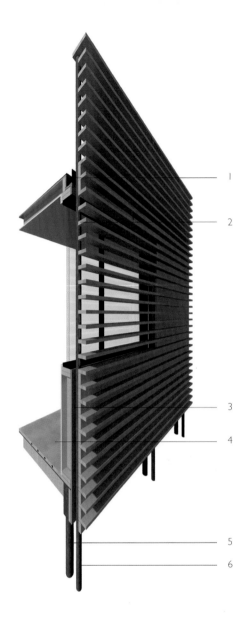

1 Integral copper gutter with downspout beyond
2 1 1/4" x 3 7/8" cedar slats
3 Exterior grade plywood
4 Concrete floor slab
5 3" composite steel pipe column
6 2" x 2" steel post

top: 3-D rendering of wall section detail
left: Front facade

Buck Creek House

Big Sur, California, projected completion date 2011

This three-bedroom vacation home on Big Sur's spectacular south coast is anchored in the natural beauty and power of the California landscape. Our design embeds the building within the land, creating a structure that is inseparable from its context. The site, which features a 250-foot drop to the Pacific Ocean along the bluff and toward the west, offers dramatic views. Yet it demands a more complex form than a giant picture window.

The long, thin volume of the house conforms to the natural contours of the land and the geometries of the bluff, deforming its shape and structure in response, much like the banana slug native to the region's seaside forests. In this way, the complex structural system applies natural forms to accommodate the siting. The main bearing system of the house is set back twelve feet from the bluff, both to protect the cliff's delicate ecosystem and to ensure the structure's integrity and safety. The house itself is cantilevered over the bluff. The interior is a shelter, an elegant refuge in contrast with the roughness and immense scale of the ocean and cliff.

The main body of the house is composed of two rectangular boxes connected by an all-glass library/den. A one-story concrete wing perpendicular to the main volume holds the ground-floor bedrooms and features a green roof; it is the boulder that locks the house to the land. The lower of the two main volumes, a double-cantilevered master bedroom suite, acts as a promontory above the ocean, offering breathtaking views from its floor-to-ceiling windows. The upper volume is an open-plan space—kitchen, living room, and dining room—with a swooping ceiling, all clad in wood, that follows the shape of the land.

The house's two main facades express both shelter and exposure. On the north, clear expanses of glass reveal ocean and coastline views; long strips of translucent channel glass dapple the light, playing on the sea's shimmering surface. The south facade, clad in copper, which wraps over the roof, is mostly enclosed, offering a retreat from the forces of nature. Roof overhangs on the east and west protect the windows and the front door from the harshness of sun and wind.

opposite
View from north

this page
Banana slug

0   32'

this page
Site, plan, and section

opposite
top: View of the site
bottom: Aerial view

overleaf
View from south

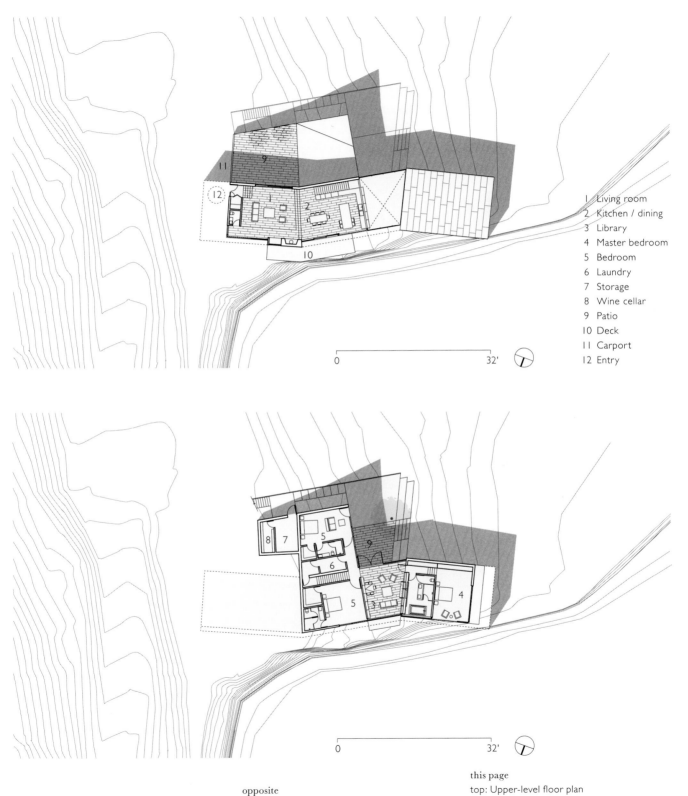

1 Living room
2 Kitchen / dining
3 Library
4 Master bedroom
5 Bedroom
6 Laundry
7 Storage
8 Wine cellar
9 Patio
10 Deck
11 Carport
12 Entry

0   32'

this page
top: Upper-level floor plan
bottom: Lower-level floor plan

109

opposite
Library

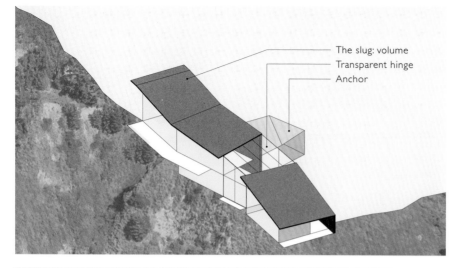

The slug: volume
Transparent hinge
Anchor

opposite
top: Conceptual diagram
middle and bottom: Context

this page
Open living, dining, and kitchen space

overleaf
Glass facade

Design/Democracy:
The Political Terrain

Art and architecture—all the arts—do not have to exist in isolation, as they do now.
This fault is very much a key to the present society. Architecture is nearly gone, but
it, art, all of the arts, in fact all parts of the society, have to be rejoined, and joined
more than they have ever been. This would be democratic in a good sense, unlike the
present increasing fragmentation into separate but equal categories, equal within the
arts, but inferior to the powerful bureaucracies.

—Donald Judd, *The Chinati Foundation: La Fundación Chinati*

Donald Judd, *The Chinati Foundation/La
Fundación Chinati* (Marfa, TX: The Chinati
Foundation, 1987), 12.

Henri Labrouste, Bibliothèque Nationale, Paris, France, 1862–68

Great architecture can, and should be, part of the political world. The new modernist's challenge is to design spaces that people use and are moved by, rather than spaces that only demonstrate theoretical constructs.

At its heart, this activist mission reconnects principles of design to principles of democracy. A building that is vivid and full of life communicates respect for all individuals within a community; an environment that is harmonious and reassuring to everyone within reinforces the value of social equality.

Creating uplifting, unconventional spaces on limited budgets is also a political act, provoking the question, "Who deserves great architecture?" A society reveals its collective answer through the clinics, offices, hospitals, libraries, community centers, and homes that its low-income citizens use and inhabit. According to democratic ideals, these buildings should reflect society's highest standards of beauty. They should delight all the senses and awaken the spirit; they should exist as perceptually rich spaces, full of the elements and phenomena most often associated with great architecture for the wealthy: light and transparency, as well as richly textured materials and details.

This vision is subversive, as it confronts the normative design vocabulary, pushes clients' expectations and aesthetics, shapes new public and private collaborations, and engages craftsmen and artists to use innovative materials and technologies. Through this vision, architecture on the political terrain does more than occupy city space with structure: it fills in urban gaps, heals urban inequities, and—especially—enhances urban life. In this type of work, the new modernist directly engages cultural assumptions about citizens' wealth and worth and rejects social pretenses.

Parkview Terraces

San Francisco, California, 2008

Fougeron Architecture was selected, after a competitive process, to resolve the many challenges inherent in this affordable, multiuse senior housing project: complex city and community reviews of design and programming; complicated financing issues; and a difficult site on a very tight former freeway location in San Francisco. Removed after the 1989 earthquake, this freeway had once split the surrounding neighborhoods, leaving economic and social scars at the prominent intersection of Turk and Gough Streets.

Each step of the project took negotiation and reinterpretation, civic action, and design innovation. We focused our vision for the 101-unit concrete and glass building on creating an open relationship between the interior spaces and their larger city context—a major design challenge. Our aim was for residents to fully participate in the life of the street, to appreciate the site's sun angles, and to enjoy views of the parks across the street and the distant hills beyond. We rejected outdated designs that would have patronized the elderly low-income residents through false quaintness or subjected them to lifeless economies.

The building's innovative massing and unit arrangement met the site's challenges and ensured affordability. The L-shaped volume engages different street-level contexts and gives all units ample natural light and park views. A nine-story tower, rising out of the first three floors of the north facade, made it possible to fit 101 units in such a tight space. The placement of the tower also allows sunlight to pour into the generous ground-floor courtyard terrace and the fourth-floor terrace to the south.

Taking advantage of the downhill cross-slope, we placed a full level of parking and storage below the Turk Street entry, allowing for ground-floor communal spaces: a double-height lobby, community room, health club, beauty salon, therapy center, social services center, and offices. Several of these amenities are accessible from the sidewalk as well as from the main lobby.

The most striking design innovation is in the north- and south-facing facades of the tower, where the traditional bay window rhythm of the San Francisco street is replaced by glassy waves. Along with the staggered, horizontal undulation of the window bays, exterior bands extend and expose the floor slabs at one- and two-story intervals, mitigating building scale and creating visual interest at no added material cost.

Undulating facade along Turk Street

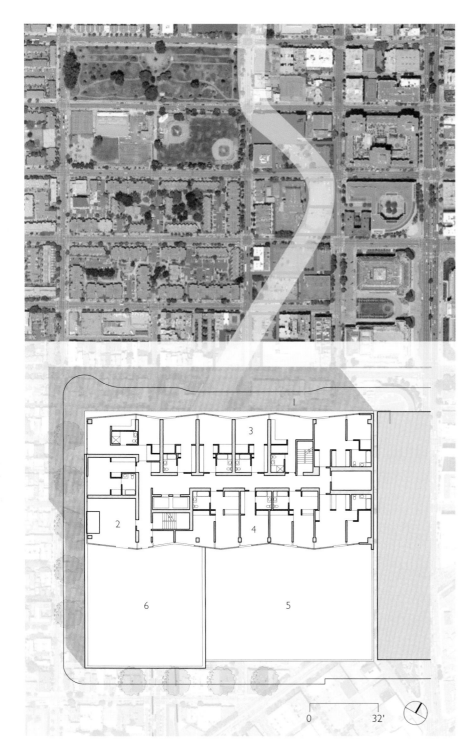

1 Entry
2 Library
3 Studio unit
4 One-bedroom unit
5 Ground-floor courtyard
6 Fourth-floor terrace

0   32'

opposite
Typical floor plan

this page
Rear courtyard roof terraces

top: Gough Street facade and roof terrace
right: Corner of Turk and Gough Streets at night

opposite
Undulating facade

this page
Main entrance

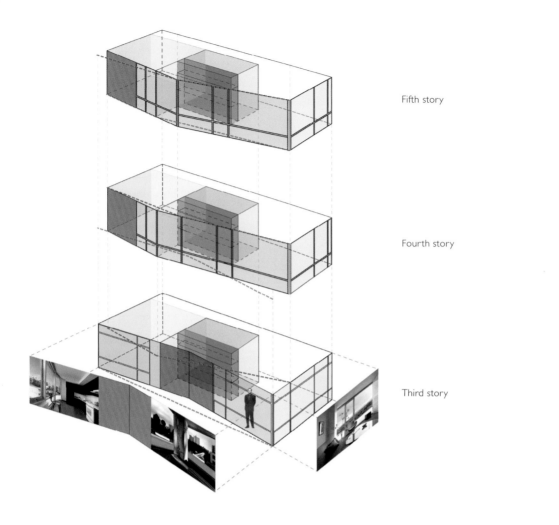

Fifth story

Fourth story

Third story

Bedroom
Bathroom
Kitchen

Planned Parenthood architecture lives in the political realm. It has to not only advance the organization's transformative mission—reproductive justice—but also protect staff and clients against serious threats of terrorism, all on the limited budget of a community-based nonprofit serving low-income citizens in the critical, culturally sensitive field of sexual and reproductive health.

Commissioned by Planned Parenthood's San Francisco Bay region affiliate, Planned Parenthood Golden Gate (PPGG), we have created health care centers and offices that refute the convention that low-cost, functional, and space-efficient environments must look antiseptic. Visually exciting and invisibly yet powerfully secure, these spaces animate personal and professional interactions with dignity, warmth, and respect.

By integrating materials that are natural and renewable with materials that are energy-efficient and technologically advanced, these modernist structures also use resources sensibly, economically, and imaginatively. Perspective, alignment, and balance are crucial elements in the composition of space.

Engaging all the senses with unusual palettes of color, light, and natural materials, our design boldly states that income should not determine access to high-quality architecture—or health care.

Eddy Street Administrative Offices

San Francisco, California, 2004

This remodel of PPGG's administrative offices revived an unremarkable seven-thousand-square-foot space, which consisted of a monotonous deep floor plate and low ceilings. From the new bold reception area to the interior workspaces and conference rooms, the offices are now filled with light, streamlined with interesting surfaces, and accented with vivid color. The design successfully serves both PPGG's high-level mission and operational objectives, balancing administrators' needs for community, privacy, and security.

Transparent and sandblasted glass along the perimeter walls open up the space and allow natural light deep into the interior. The office walls glow day and night, creating an abstract, luminous background for the custom steel workstations. Finely detailed and crafted, these cubicles are clad with wood slats, heightening the impression of transparency and introducing a tactile quality to ordinary office space. Canted overhead canopies of steel and sandblasted glass break up the plane of the T-bar ceiling and soften the artificial fluorescent lighting above.

Core and communal functions are housed in free-standing volumes that are partially clad in gypsum board and painted a bright red. Sandblasted clerestories bring light into these spaces, and black steel bands at the top create continuity with the steel workstations. The red wall behind the reception desk serves as a brilliant backdrop for the organization's mission statement, silk-screened on Plexiglas, calling attention to PPGG's fundamental commitment to reproductive justice.

Individual workstations

1   Entry
2   Reception
3   Conference room
4   Workstations
5   Lounge

0   16'

opposite
top: Custom-built workstations
bottom: Floor plan

this page
Offices along main corridor

opposite

Wood perforated privacy screen

this page

Workstations

MacArthur Health Center

Oakland, California, 2004

PPGG's commitment to high-quality health care for this economically depressed, culturally diverse Oakland neighborhood challenged us to completely remodel the interior and exterior of a two-story, seven-thousand-square-foot building into a modern clinic. Complex programmatic and political issues demanded solutions on a shoestring budget.

Our strategy took a unified approach to opposing goals: to increase security against terrorist threats and to express warmth and welcome to PPGG's staff and patients. The resulting dynamic design rebuts common wisdom that says medical facilities must look drab—particularly those built with limited funds for low-income patients.

Although organized in a typical U-shaped plan, the clinic's spaces are articulated in an unconventional way. Four large central volumes with dramatically canted walls, skylights, and a courtyard flood the interior with natural light. In the smaller spaces within the larger canted volumes, light entering from the skylights above bounces off richly painted roofs onto the white corridor walls. This colored refracted light, which changes in hue and intensity throughout the day, is a constant reminder of the exterior world beyond.

Clinic corridors act as streets for easy, efficient interaction between patients and staff. Sophisticated geometric steel accents play off the softness of the corridors' frosted glass walls and windows that evoke greater openness. Economical in operation and maintenance, the clinic nonetheless incorporates handcrafted, homelike details and textures that express architecture's sensual qualities. Visually interesting, durable, and tactile materials such as cork, wood paneling, and rice-paper laminates are used throughout. Humor also comes into play in the form of candy jars filled with colored condoms—an amusing reminder of the importance of safe sex.

We saw the required security upgrade as an opportunity to enhance the beauty and functionality of the clinic rather than turn it into a fortress. New security measures, such as bullet-resistant desk enclosures and walls, were unobtrusively integrated into the design, fully supporting PPGG's mission to make women's health centers as safe, welcoming, and accessible as possible.

Located near the reception desk, a small garden courtyard provides a serene visual oasis for both staff and patients. Its peaceful design is the heart of this busy clinic.

opposite
Courtyard

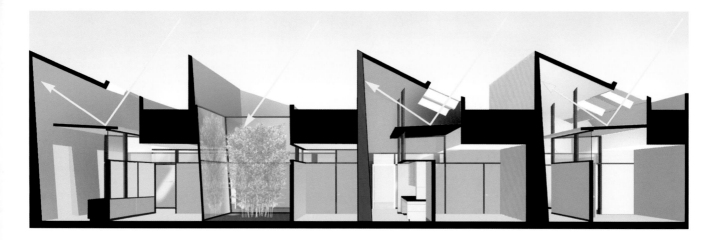

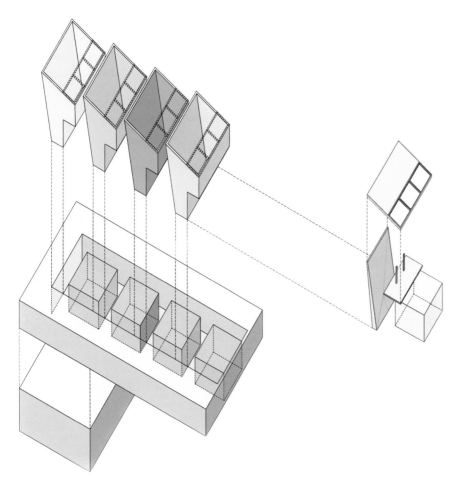

this page
top: Diagram showing refracted colored
    light on white walls with changing hues
bottom: Axonometric of skylights

opposite
View along corridor

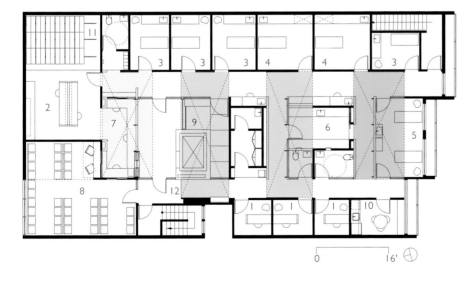

1	Office
2	Workstations
3	Exam rooms
4	Exam / surgery
5	Recovery
6	Lab
7	Reception
8	Waiting room
9	Courtyard
10	Staff lounge
11	Files
12	Entry

0   16'

opposite
Reception area

this page
left: Bench and candy jars
right: Bench
bottom: Floor plan

Culture/Context:
Twenty-First-Century Civitas

We shape our buildings, thereafter, they shape us.

—Sir Winston Churchill

From speech by Churchill to House of Commons,
Oct. 28, 1943.

Victor Louis, Jardin du Palais-Royal, Paris, France, 1784

What is the purpose of public space in this age of hypercommunication? For many of us, our essential common ground has become virtual, and our cultural landscape is defined by specs, screens, and applications. But even as we are invisibly drawn tighter together within this networked world, we are also physically linked in extremely complex and heterogeneous urban centers. Forty years from now, nearly 80 percent of the world's population will live in increasingly dense urban environments. In this new social landscape, public architecture must act as the operating system of civic life, sustaining culture and learning, renewing housing and agriculture, and creating community.

Temples of elitism, classic structures of isolated culture, are already falling. Taking their place are innovative urban structures connected to the life of the street and designed to raise the social spirit and economic vitality of the city. These buildings engage people—with each other, with information, and with the creation and transmission of culture. They also use land sparingly and imaginatively. The conversion of existing urban spaces for new uses defines twenty-first-century civitas. Remodeling is not a second-tier architectural challenge anymore; rather, it is at the leading edge of design innovation—an expression of green policy and values.

With this shift, urbanism and environmentalism are no longer considered opposing forces. They can be aligned in sustainable designs that support new forms of commerce, transportation, and agriculture, putting invention in the service of community and claiming a new common ground.

Ingleside Branch Library

San Francisco, California, 2009

Winner of a national competition, our design uplifts the community library's traditional role as a temple of knowledge while modernizing its personality as a digital-age center of independent learning. A gathering place for the diverse population of San Francisco's Ingleside neighborhood, the library's animated facade announces the vibrant community life within.

Facing a heavily commercial street, the L-shaped building adheres to the urban grid. Two large, independently floating forms frame its main entry: the boxy volume of the library's program room and the egg shape of the children's reading room—the composition's focal point. The reading room's bay window—a glowing beacon of glass—advertises the value and accessibility of literacy for all.

A high canopy roof, hovering twenty feet above the entrance, creates an iconic profile for the one-story structure, establishing its civic presence and distinction on the street as a public building. The canopy's blue underside, a virtual second sky, is uplit at night, subtly communicating the library's message of ambition and aspiration.

Within are four distinct groups of spaces. In addition to the children's reading room, the main reading room is a grand-scale public hall that speaks to the classical model of libraries. Its sculpted ceiling pours in light from above through dramatic skylights. Quiet, intimate carrels for reading, relaxing, and computer use face a rear courtyard and garden, allowing both indoor/outdoor flow and flexibility for the library's potential expansion. Diffuse light—filtered through the wood and glass ceiling and through sun-shaded windows—creates a quiet ambiance. Finally, the services gallery (consisting of the workroom, manager's office, and staff lounge) essentially forms a separate wing facing a residential street. This placement buffers the learning spaces and provides professional, private workspaces for the staff.

Throughout, durable eco-friendly materials lower maintenance costs while providing visual and tactile delights. Metal louvers and sunshades, mahogany-framed study nooks, tile, and glass all give the library a beauty appropriate to its high civic purpose.

opposite
Main entrance on Ocean Avenue

this page
Second-sky roof

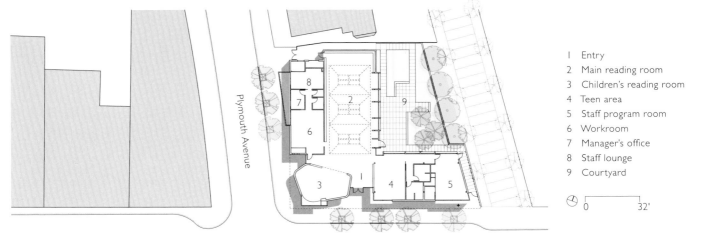

1 Entry
2 Main reading room
3 Children's reading room
4 Teen area
5 Staff program room
6 Workroom
7 Manager's office
8 Staff lounge
9 Courtyard

0   32'

Plymouth Avenue

Ocean Avenue

opposite
Floor plan

above
Front facade

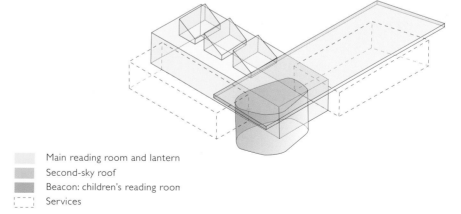

Main reading room and lantern
Second-sky roof
Beacon: children's reading roon
Services

opposite
Exterior view of egg-shaped children's
reading room

this page
top: Second-sky roof
bottom: Diagram: composition

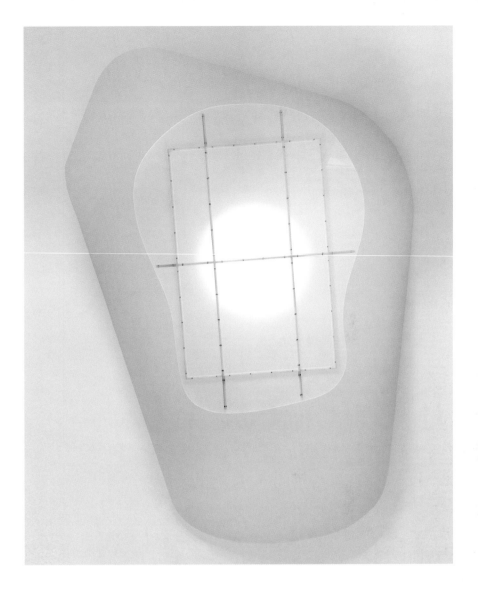

opposite
Children's reading room, interior

this page
Children's reading room, ceiling

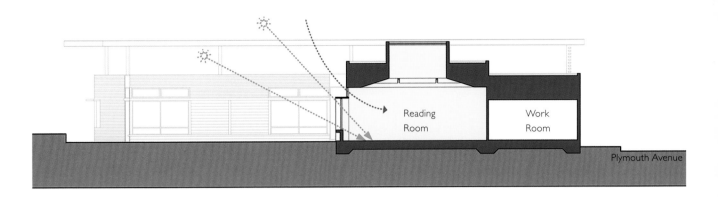

Reading Room

Work Room

Plymouth Avenue

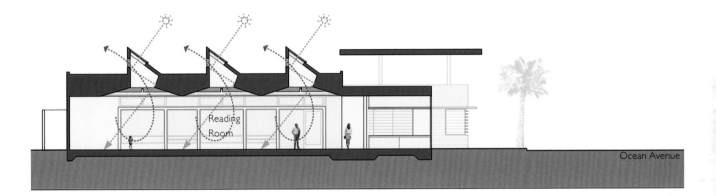

Reading Room

Ocean Avenue

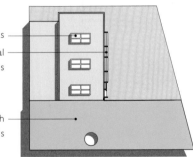

Louvered lantern skylights

Sunshaded, operable windows: natural light and ventilation in all rooms

Second-sky roof with photovoltaic panels

Natural light

Natural ventilation

opposite
Main reading room

this page
top: Sections: natural daylight and ventilation
bottom: Diagram: natural daylight and sustainable features

overleaf
Teen room and lobby

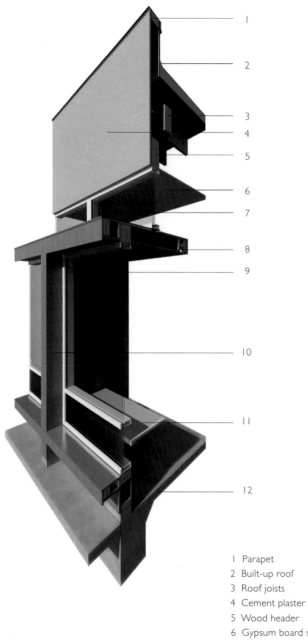

1 Parapet
2 Built-up roof
3 Roof joists
4 Cement plaster
5 Wood header
6 Gypsum board suspended ceiling
7 Steel pipe column
8 Fluorescent light fixture
9 Aluminum window system
10 Mahogany siding
11 Solid surface countertop
12 Concrete footing and slab

previous spread
Courtyard

this page
3-D rendering of window wall

opposite
Study carrels

opposite
Main reading room from teen room

this page
View along circulation axis

overleaf
Ocean Avenue facade at night

Hosfelt Gallery

San Francisco, California, 2000

Commissioned by the owner to create a space in which to build the expanding business and the growing international reputation of the Hosfelt Gallery, we converted an industrial warehouse into an upscale exhibition, work, and storage space that accommodates more artists, clients, and inventory than the gallery's previous space. Transforming the concrete-frame building presented two main challenges: to create a minimalist yet lively gallery space and a visually dramatic yet inexpensive entrance.

Leaving the exterior untouched, we recast the still-functional loading dock as a glowing, open-air entry. Sandblasted glass panels—weather- and graffiti-proof—are held in place with custom steel brackets and backlit with continuous strips of neon light. This passageway of smooth, reflective glass vividly connects the two contrasting spaces of the rough alley without and the refined gallery within. Ingeniously differentiating old from new, street from inner sanctum, its design calls attention to both the nature of urban culture and art-viewing itself. Gallery visitors walking up the light-filled ramp are themselves momentarily seen as objects on display.

The interior holds three viewing rooms: a main gallery for large works, a smaller one for photographs and works on paper, and a windowless gallery for video art. Administrative functions are placed along the front facade, shielding the exhibition spaces from direct sunlight. The opposition of old and new acts as the organizational principle. Simple white gypsum board walls—kept separate from the existing structure throughout—float as abstract planes in an otherwise unadorned space. Existing concrete columns are also kept separate from the new walls and ceiling, creating a liquid space that revitalizes the building without changing its character. The viewer's eye is in constant motion, as walls break and turn corners, exposing the art and the people on display from a multitude of angles.

The gallery's integration of building technology and art, texture and light, space and dimension has encouraged an increasing number of diverse and internationally acclaimed artists to present work at Hosfelt. Some even create with the space in mind, in conversation with the gallery's continuous visual vocabulary.

opposite
Main entrance

this page
Entrance at night

top: Glass support detail
right: Entrance and gallery beyond

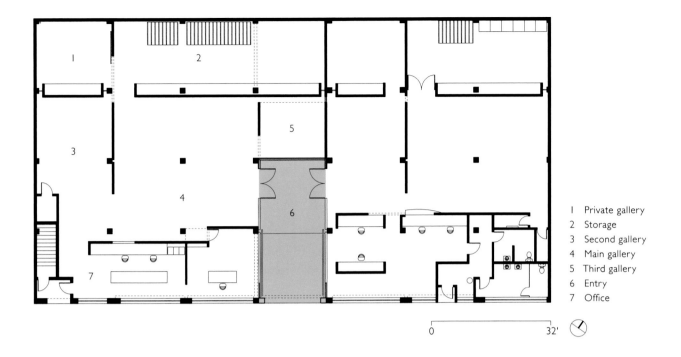

1   Private gallery
2   Storage
3   Second gallery
4   Main gallery
5   Third gallery
6   Entry
7   Office

0   32'

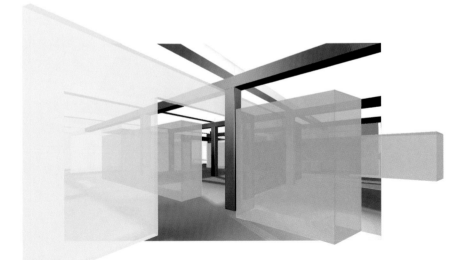

opposite
Gallery space

this page
top: Floor plan
bottom: New walls are kept separate from
existing walls, columns, and ceiling.

top: Small gallery space
right: Main gallery space

City of the Future

San Francisco, California, 2008

Imagine urban life in one hundred years. Over ten billion people worldwide will be straining for limited resources of water, land, and food. More than 80 percent of the world's population will be living in dense urban centers, and one of the main issues that will have to be solved is how they will be fed. Today's agricultural model has no answer, with 80 percent of land suitable for raising crops already in use. At worst, as resources become increasingly scarce, the tense edge between city and farm could become a battle line.

In 2008, we were given one week to conceive a new balance of urbanism, technology, and ecology in the City of the Future competition sponsored by the History Channel, IBM, and Infiniti, with the American Institute of Architects and American Society of Civil Engineers as partners. We advanced a future vision of San Francisco as a model sustainable city, with agriculture woven directly into its urban framework. Drawing on the research of Dickson Despommier, a professor of environmental health sciences and microbiology at Columbia University who developed the Vertical Farm Project, we deployed vertical agricultural systems, fed by reclaimed water and powered through renewable energy technologies, throughout the Bay Area region.

By reappropriating existing structures and developing new agricultural centers along key nodes of the regional transportation network, this model cultivates an urban environment that is directly linked to its food supply and is agriculturally self-sufficient. Food can be produced and distributed with high efficiency, and gone are the costly environmental effects of the outmoded industrial agricultural model. A new base of industry, producing a safe, varied food supply, takes its place in an increasingly dense, stratified city.

This projection is not an idle exercise. Forces of climate change, high energy cost, globalization, and urbanization are all converging to press for better systems of food production, distribution, and consumption. As global food demand and prices are rising, new areas of hunger are steadily emerging in developing countries, and even middle-class city dwellers are being priced out of the food market.

Solutions must come from architects with a social conscience. Committed to food equity and universal public health, they can lead a new type of civitas through urban vision and renewal.

Vertical and rooftop farming in San Francisco, 2108

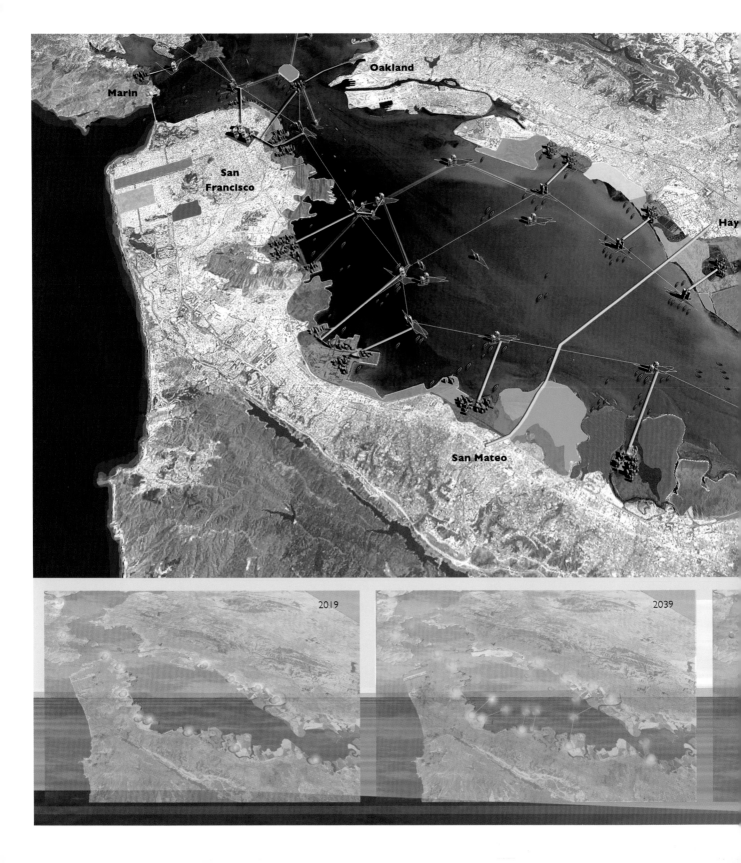

Marin

Oakland

San
Francisco

Hay

San Mateo

2019

2039

FACTS AND FIGURES:

- As of 2008, 80 percent of the land suitable for raising crops was already in use.
- By 2051, 80 percent of the world's population will reside in urban centers, pushing urban edges further out into neighboring agricultural land.
- By 2108, there will be ten billion people in the world.
- *Where will we find the farmland we need? How will we feed ourselves?*

- Food prices are estimated to increase by 35 percent in coming years.
- Income growth, climate change, high energy prices, globalization, and urbanization are all converging to transform how food is produced, marketed, and consumed.
- Global food demand and prices are rising, threatening the livelihoods and nutrition of poor people in all countries.
- A "new area of hunger" is emerging in developing countries; even middle-class urbanites are being priced out of the food market due to rising costs.

- Agriculture uses 70 percent of the world's available freshwater for irrigation, rendering it unusable for drinking as a result of contamination with fertilizers, pesticides, herbicides, and silt.
- Forty percent of the world's food production occurs on irrigated land.

- Americans import $52.5 billion worth of agricultural products each year.
- Food in the United States travels an average of 1,726 miles from farm to market.

- All-season farming multiplies the productivity of the farmed surface by a factor of four to six, depending on the crop.
- A thirty-story building with a base of a building block (five acres) could produce yields analogous to that of a traditional 2,400-acre farm if year-round and special genetic "dwarf" crops are used.
- Vertical farming could eventually replace traditional farmlands, thus restoring them to their natural state and preventing further desertification, deforestation, and invasion of natural biomes. Farms are a leading cause of animal habitat loss and extinctions, particularly in developing countries. Each acre in a vertical farm could allow between ten and twenty acres of traditional farmland to return to its natural state.

top: Site plan: a new network of agricultural towers and piers
bottom: Evolution of urban agriculture

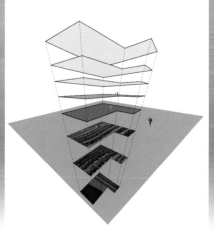

Apples
Tomatoes
Artichokes
Carrots
Onions
Peppers
Lettuce
Asparagus

Vertical Farms

Variety of crops grown at specific levels of unused garage

Underground Farms

In 2108, with cars banned from the city, millions of unused garage square footage will become urban farm powered by solar panels and wind turbines, irrigated by gray water from floors above.

Roof Gardens

Use existing flat roofs as urban agricultural space and platforms for solar panel arrays

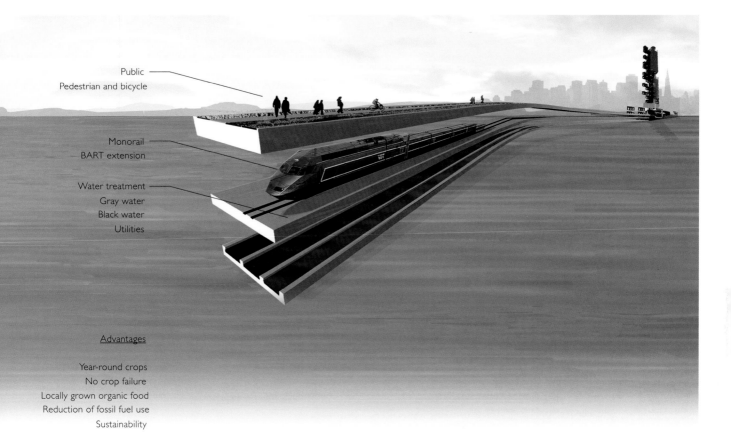

Public
Pedestrian and bicycle

Monorail
BART extension

Water treatment
Gray water
Black water
Utilities

Advantages

Year-round crops
No crop failure
Locally grown organic food
Reduction of fossil fuel use
Sustainability

opposite
top: Vertical farms, underground farms, and
   roof gardens
bottom: Sustainable skyline

this page
Public transportation system

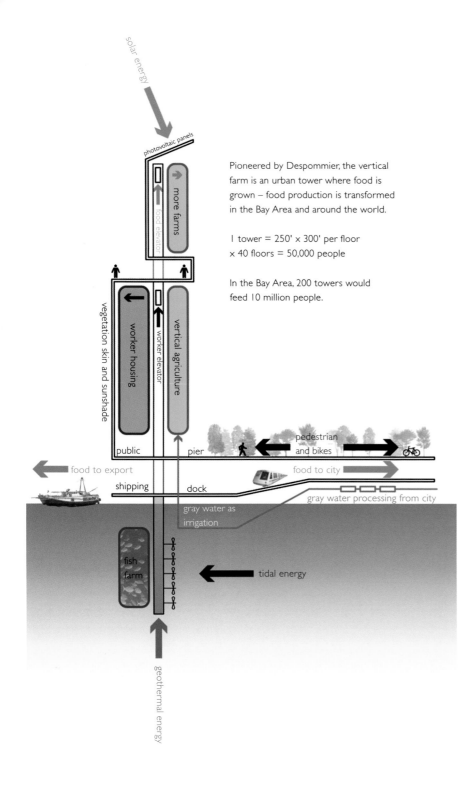

solar energy

photovoltaic panels

more farms

food elevator

Pioneered by Despommier, the vertical farm is an urban tower where food is grown – food production is transformed in the Bay Area and around the world.

1 tower = 250' × 300' per floor × 40 floors = 50,000 people

In the Bay Area, 200 towers would feed 10 million people.

vegetation skin and sunshade

worker housing

worker elevator

vertical agriculture

public

pier

pedestrian and bikes

food to export

food to city

shipping

dock

gray water processing from city

gray water as irrigation

fish farm

tidal energy

geothermal energy

this page
Agricultural towers

opposite
Agricultural tower providing housing
and food production

overleaf
New self-sufficient city center and waterfront

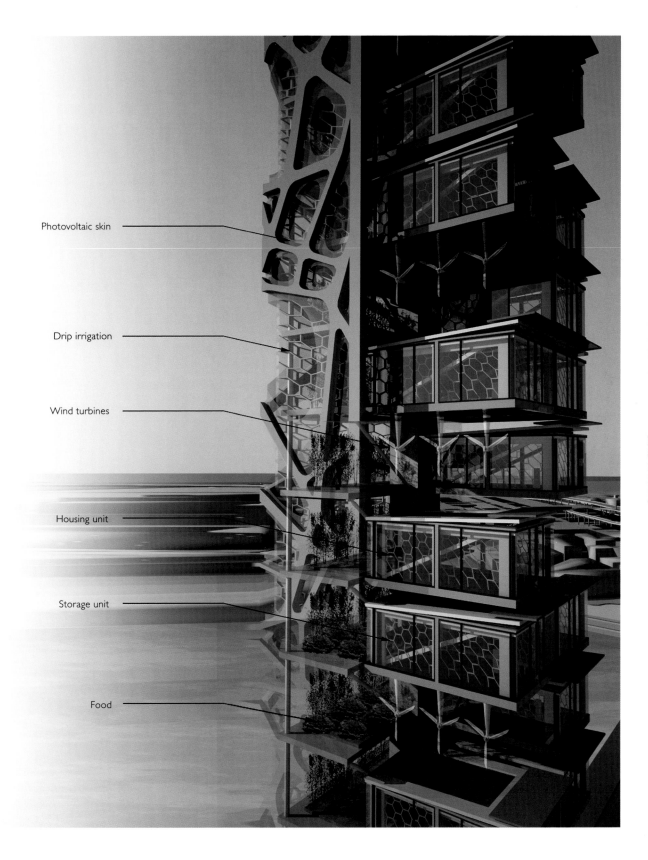

Photovoltaic skin

Drip irrigation

Wind turbines

Housing unit

Storage unit

Food

Project Credits

1532 House (San Francisco, California, 2006)

Awards: AIA Housing Award, 2007; AIA San Francisco Honor
    Award, 2007; Custom Home Design Award, 2007; AIA East Bay
    Honor Award, 2006; Award of Excellence, Society of American
    Registered Architects, New York Council, 2006; AIA California
    Council Merit Award, 2006

Project Architect: Anne Fougeron
Project Team: Todd Aranaz, Michael Pierry, Ethen Wood, Ryan
    Murphy, Anne Tipp
General Contractor: Peter Harris Construction
Landscape Architect: Lutsko Associates
Structural Engineer: Endres Ware LLP
Photography: Richard Barnes

21 House (San Francisco, California, 2002)

Project Architect: Anne Fougeron
Project Team: Todd Aranaz, Russell Sherman, Michael Pierry
General Contractor: Young & Burton
Structural Engineer: Endres Ware LLP
Metal Fabricator: Dennis Luedeman
Photography: Grey Crawford, Matthew Millman

440 House (Palo Alto, California, 1999)

Awards: AIA Best of the Bay and Beyond Award, 2001; DuPont
    Benedictus Glass Award, 2000

Project Architect: Anne Fougeron
Project Team: Russell Sherman, Todd Aranaz, Cathleen Chua
    Schulte, Addison Strong, Christine Kiesling, Elizabeth Garcia
General Contractor: Young & Burton
Landscape Architect: Topher Delaney
Structural Engineer: Endres Ware LLP
Photography: Tim Street-Porter, Richard Barnes

Fuel Lounge (Akron, Ohio, 2004)

Project Architect: Anne Fougeron
Project Team: Todd Aranaz, Anne Tipp
Mechanical, Electrical, and Plumbing: TM Westover Architects
Photography: Albert Vecerka

Tehama Grasshopper (San Francisco, California, 2008)

Awards: Best of California Home and Design Award, Residential
    Architecture, 2009; AIA East Bay Exceptional Residential Honor
    Award, 2008; AIA San Francisco Excellence in Architecture
    Honor Award, 2008; Custom Home Design Merit Award, 2008;
    AIA Institute Honor Award for Interior Architecture, 2008;
    Residential Architect Grand Design Award, 2008; AIA California
    Council Merit Award, 2007

Project Architect: Anne Fougeron
Project Team: Todd Aranaz, Ryan Jang, Angela Thomason, Toby
    Stewart
General Contractor: Johnstone McAuliffe Construction
Structural Engineer: Endres Ware LLP
Metal Fabricator: Dennis Luedeman
Photography: Richard Barnes, Matthew Millman
Rendering: Jacek Gaczynski

Jackson Family Retreat (Big Sur, California, 2005)

Awards: AIA East Bay Honor Award, 2006; Merit Award,
    International Interior Design Association, Northern California
    Chapter, 2006; AIA California Council Honor Award, 2005; AIA
    San Francisco Excellence in Architecture Merit Award, 2005;
    Record House Award, Architectural Record magazine, 2005

Project Architect: Anne Fougeron
Project Team: Todd Aranaz, Russell Sherman, Michael Pierry, Anne
    Tipp, Vivian Dwyer, Ethen Wood, Ryan Murphy
General Contractor: Thomas George Construction
Civil Engineer: Harold Grice, Grice Engineering & Geology
Structural Engineer: Endres Ware LLP
Facilitator: Arden Handshy
Biological Engineer: Jeff Norman
Forester: Webster & Associates
Archaeological Services: Archaeological Resource Management
Photography: Richard Barnes

Buck Creek House (Big Sur, California, projected completion date 2011)

Project Architect: Anne Fougeron
Project Team: Todd Aranaz, Ryan Jang, Angela Thomason, Ted Rzad
General Contractor: Thomas George Construction
Landscape Architect: Blasen Landscape Architecture
Civil Engineer: Grice Engineering & Geology
Structural Engineer: Endres Ware LLP
Facilitator: Arden Handshy
Rendering: Jacek Gaczynski

Parkview Terraces (San Francisco, California, 2008)

Awards: AIA East Bay Merit Award, 2009; Readers' Choice Award, *Affordable Housing Finance* Magazine, 2009; Multi-Housing News Design Excellence Award, Honorable Mention, 2008; Gold Nugget Merit Award, 2008

Project Architect: Kwan Henmi Architecture/Planning
Project Team: Sylvia Kwan, Robert Jansen, Ana Paula, Janet MacKinnor
Consulting Architect: Fougeron Architecture
Project Team: Anne Fougeron, Bassel Samaha, Todd Aranaz, Michael Pierry, Toby Stewart
General Contractor: Cahill Contractors
Landscape Architect: Stevens & Associates
Civil Engineer: Telamon Engineering Consultants
Structural Engineer: Forell/Elsesser Engineers
Mechanical and Plumbing: SJ Engineering
Electrical Engineer: F. W. Associates
Photography: Joe Fletcher, Rien van Rijthoven

Planned Parenthood Golden Gate, Eddy Street Administrative Offices (San Francisco, California, 2004)

Project Architect: Anne Fougeron
Project Team: Todd Aranaz
General Contractor: Jetton Construction
Photography: Matthew Millman

Planned Parenthood Golden Gate, San Mateo Call Center (San Mateo, California, 2002)

Awards: AIA San Mateo Design Award Citation, 2003

Project Architect: Anne Fougeron
Project Team: Michael Pierry, Anne Tipp, Vivian Dwyer, Ryan Murphy
General Contractor: Jetton Construction
Structural Engineer: Jon Brody Structural Engineers
Metal Fabricator: Dennis Luedeman
Lighting: Dan Dodt
Acoustical Engineer: Charles M. Salter
Photography: Matthew Millman

Planned Parenthood Golden Gate, MacArthur Health Center (Oakland, California, 2004)

Awards: Honor Award, International Interior Design Association, New York Chapter, 2005; AIA San Francisco Excellence in Design, Merit Award, 2004; AIA East Bay Excellence in Design, Merit Award, 2003

Project Architect: Anne Fougeron
Project Team: Todd Aranaz, Ryan Murphy, Michael Pierry, Anne Tipp
General Contractor: BBI Construction
Structural Engineer: Jon Brody Structural Engineers
Metal Fabricator: Dennis Luedeman
Lighting: Dan Dodt
Photography: Grey Crawford

Ingleside Branch Library (San Francisco, California, 2009)

Awards: First Prize and Commission for a New Branch Library, Ingleside Library Competition, 2003

Project Architect: Anne Fougeron
Project Team: Todd Aranaz, Bassel Samaha, Michael Pierry, Ryan Jang, Vivian Dwyer, Ted Rzad
Associate Architect: Group 4 Architecture, Research + Planning
Project Team: Wayne Gehrke, David Schnee, Prasasti Arief
General Contractor: CLW Builders
Landscape Architect: Patricia O'Brien Landscape Architecture
Civil Engineer: Telamon Engineering Consultants
Structural Engineer: Ingraham DeJesse Associates
Mechanical Engineer: G. M. Lim & Associates
Electrical Engineer: Pola Design + Engineering
Technology Consultant: Smith, Fause & McDonald
Rendering: Zendarski Studio
Public Artwork: Eric Powell
Photography: Joe Fletcher

Hosfelt Gallery (San Francisco, California, 2000)

Awards: AIA Best of the Bay and Beyond Award, 2001

Project Architect: Anne Fougeron
Project Team: Todd Aranaz, Vivian Dwyer, Russell Sherman
General Contractor: Jetton Construction
Structural Engineer: Endres Ware LLP
Metal Fabricator: Dennis Luedeman
Lighting: Dan Dodt
Photography: Ethan Kaplan, Jay Jones

City of the Future (San Francisco, California, 2008)

Awards: Infiniti Design Excellence Award, City of the Future Competition, sponsored by the History Channel, IBM, and Infiniti, with the AIA and American Society of Civil Engineers as partners, 2008

Project Architect: Anne Fougeron
Project Team: Todd Aranaz, Ryan Jang, Sean Bailey, Matt Goodwin, Francisco Maravilla, Rade Radakovic, Scott Rothi
Rendering: Sean Bailey

Select Bibliography

Asensio, Francisco. *American Houses*. New York: Atrium Group, 2009. (1532 House, 440 House, and Jackson Family Retreat)

Bell, Victoria Ballard, and Patrick Rand. "440 House." In *Materials for Design*. New York: Princeton Architectural Press, 2006.

Berton, Monica, Helen Cooney, and Susan Page. "1532 House" and "Jackson Family Retreat." In *Home: New Directions in World Architecture and Design*. Cincinnati, OH: HOW Books, 2006.

Caldwell, Kenneth. "Architectural Opportunities in Design for Aging." *arcCa* (February 2009): 16–21. (Parkview Terraces)

Chatfield-Taylor, Joan. "Wild Imagination." *Design for Living* (Spring 2007): 78–83. (Jackson Family Retreat)

Clay, Rebecca. "Integrating Security & Design." *ASID ICON* (Spring 2005): 36–41. (Planned Parenthood Golden Gate and MacArthur Health Center)

Futagawa, Yoshio, ed. "Big Sur House." In *GA Houses: Residential Masterpieces*. Vol. 89. Tokyo: A.D.A. Edita Tokyo Co., 2005. (Jackson Family Retreat)

Hospitality Design. "Fuel Lounge." April 2005, 34.

King, John. "No One Knows What Our City Will Look Like in 2108. But Why Not Have Fun Imagining?" *San Francisco Chronicle*, January 29, 2008.

———. "Top Planner Picks Favorite Buildings. 1532 Cole Street. Fougeron Architecture 2005." *San Francisco Chronicle*, March 16, 2009.

Kliczkowski, Hugo. "Jackson Retreat." In *Exclusive Houses/Casas Exclusivas: Sea & Mountain/Mar y Montaña*. Barcelona: LOFT Publications, 2006.

Lassell, Michael. *Glamour: Making It Modern*. New York: Filipacchi, 2009. (Tehama Grasshopper)

Lee, Lydia. "Light House." *California Home + Design* (October 2006): 124–31. (1532 House)

Malinowski, Michael. "Affordable Senior Housing as an Engine for Urban Revitalization." *arcCa* (February 2009): 30–35. (Parkview Terraces)

Maury, Cecil. "Greenhouse Effect." *Perspective* (Hong Kong) (April 2008): 38–42. (Tehama Grasshopper)

McLeod, Virginia. "Fougeron Architecture: Jackson Family Retreat, USA." In *Detail in Contemporary Residential Architecture*. London: Laurence King Publishing, 2007.

Mueller, Balz, and Mark Donohue, eds. *5 x 2: Research and the Making of Architecture*. CCA Architecture Studio Series. San Francisco, CA: California College of the Arts/William Stout Publishers/University of California Berkeley, 2006. (Jackson Family Retreat)

Pearson, Clifford A. "Kwan Henmi and Anne Fougeron Give Senior Housing a Hip New Look at Parkview Terraces." *Architectural Record* (October 2008): 200–203.

Rapp, Alan. "Force of Nature." *San Francisco Magazine* (December 2005): 128–33. (Jackson Family Retreat)

Sardar, Zahid. "The Glass Menage." *San Francisco Examiner Magazine* (February 2000): 10–13. (440 House)

———. "Nature Preserved." *San Francisco Chronicle Magazine* (November 2005): 12–17. (Jackson Family Retreat)

Schwarzer, Mitchell. "Encounters with Light." *California Homes* (February 2007): 76–79. (Jackson Family Retreat and 1532 House)

———. "25 House: Fougeron Architecture." In *San Francisco: Architecture of the San Francisco Bay Area: A History & Guide*. San Francisco, CA: William Stout Publishers, 2006. (1532 House)

Stephens, Suzanne. "Big Sur House." *Architectural Record: Record Houses 2005* (April 2005): 188–93. (Jackson Family Retreat)

———. "Not Only Zaha." *Architectural Record* (December 2006): 58–68. (1532 House)

"Tehama Grasshopper." *INA International New Architecture* (Hong Kong) (August 2008): 70–83.

Victoria, Susan Tyree, and Diane Dorrans Saeks. "Urban Eco-tecture." *Metropolitan Home* (April 2008): 130–39. (Tehama Grasshopper)

Weaving, Andrew. "Good Design Aesthetics." In *The Home Modernised*. Edited by Jacqui Small. London: Jacqui Small LLP/Aurum Press Ltd, 2005: 44–47. (21 House)

Webb, Michael. "Jackson Family Retreat." In *Art Invention House*.
New York: Rizzoli, 2005.

————. "Treading Lightly." *Architectural Review* (March 2006): 52–55.
(Jackson Family Retreat)

Weber, Cheryl. "A Passion for Craft." *Residential Architect*
(September–October 2007): 56–64.

————. "Steel Sky." *Residential Architect* (September–October
2008): 64. (Tehama Grasshopper)

————. "10 Architects Making a Difference: Anne Fougeron,
Innovative Design." *Residential Architect* (June 2006): 60–61.
(Jackson Family Retreat and 1532 House)

Yelavich, Susan. "Fougeron Architecture: Planned Parenthood
MacArthur Clinic." In *Contemporary World Interiors*. New
York: Phaidon, 2007.

Office Credits

Fougeron Architecture Staff, 1986–2010
Alexandra Albinus
Todd Aranaz
Sean Bailey
Andy Clark
Vivian Dwyer
Brian Friel
Elizabeth Garcia
Marta Grey
Ryan Jang
Christine Kiesling
Dwight Long
Beth Mitchell
Whitney Moon
Ryan Murphy
Dan Oakley
David Ogorzalek
Brian Padgett
Patrick Pick
Michael Pierry
Ted Rzad
Deborah Saenz
Bassel Samaha
Cathleen Chua Schulte
Russell Sherman
Jamie Smith
Toby Stewart
Addison Strong
Angela Thomason
Anne Tipp
Catherine Tumanguil
Ethen Wood

Collaborator
Clare C. Novak, writer and editor, Novak Editing Services

Biography

Anne Fougeron, FAIA, is principal of Fougeron Architecture in San Francisco, California (www.fougeron.com). Born of French parents and raised in Paris and New York, she credits her bicultural upbringing as the source of her aesthetic values, which combine a respect for historic precedent with an interest in melding old and new. After earning a bachelor of arts degree in architectural history at Wellesley College and a master of architecture degree at the University of California, Berkeley, she worked for San Francisco architect and urban designer Daniel Solomon for three years, an experience that informed her awareness of the interplay between buildings and the urban environment. In 1986 she founded Fougeron Architecture and went on to design award-winning private- and public-sector projects in a decidedly modernist vocabulary. Fougeron has taught architectural design to undergraduate and graduate students at the California College of the Arts in San Francisco and the University of California, Berkeley, where she served as the Howard Friedman Visiting Professor of Professional Practice in the Department of Architecture from 2003 to 2004.